Alligators

By Stephanie Fitzgerald

Children's Press®

An Imprint of Scholastic Inc.

Content Consultant
Becky Ellsworth
Curator, Shores Region
Columbus Zoo and Aquarium

Library of Congress Cataloging-in-Publication Data

Names: Fitzgerald, Stephanie, author.
Title: Alligators/by Stephanie Fitzgerald.
Description: New York, NY: Children's Press, an imprint of Scholastic Inc., 2019. | Series: Nature's children |
Includes bibliographical references and index.
Identifiers: LCCN 2018002688| ISBN 9780531192610 (library binding) |
ISBN 9780531137543 (paperback)
Subjects: LCSH: Alligators—Juvenile literature.
Classification: LCC QL666.C925 F59 2019 | DDC 597.98/4—dc23
LC record available at https://lccn.loc.gov/2018002688

Design by Anna Tunick Tabachnik

Creative Direction: Judith E. Christ for Scholastic

Produced by Spooky Cheetah Press

Scholastic Inc., 557 Broadway, New York, NY 10012.

Photos ©: cover: Heidi and Hans-Juergen Koch/Minden Pictures; 1: Eric Isselee/Shutterstock; 4 leaf silo and throughout: stockgraphicdesigns.com; 4 top: Jim McMahon/Mapman ®; 5 alligator silo and throughout: Ace_Create/iStockphoto; 5 child silo: All-Silhouettes.com; 5 bottom: Clayton Bownds/Caters News Agency; 6 silo and throughout: Winner Studio/Shutterstock; 7: Mark Andrew Thomas/Alamy Images; 8: TopFoto/Longhurst/The Image Works; 11: Ryan.R.Smith.87/Shutterstock; 12: Photography by Alexandra Rudge/Getty Images; 15: reptiles4all/Shutterstock; 17: Arco Images GmbH/Alamy Images; 18 top left: Don Mammoser/Shutterstock; 18 top right: N_u_T/Shutterstock; 18 bottom left: Robert Hamilton/Alamy Images; 18 bottom right: roc8jas/Getty Images; 20: Norman Bateman/Dreamstime; 23: eyfoto/Getty Images; 24: Jason Ross/age fotostock;27: Robert Llewellyn/Getty Images; 28: W. Treat Davidson/Science Source; 31: Lynn M. Stone/Minden Pictures; 32: pernsanitfoto/Shutterstock; 35: Science History Images/Alamy Images; 36: Michael and Patricia Fogden/Minden Pictures; 39: Peter Weimann/age fotostock; 40: Elizabeth Pratt/Alamy Images; 42 left: Ermolaev Alexander/Shutterstock; 42 center: nevodka/Shutterstock; 42 right: Troscha/Shutterstock; 43 top left: metha1819/Shutterstock; 43 top right: Steve Byland/Shutterstock; 43 bottom left: nattanan726/Shutterstock; 43 bottom right: reptiles4all/Shutterstock.

Table of Contents

Fact File: Alligators

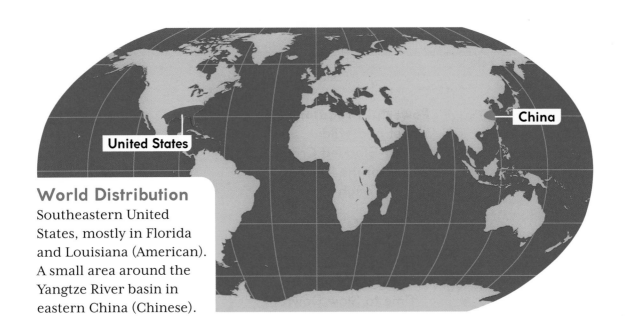

China

United States

World Distribution
Southeastern United States, mostly in Florida and Louisiana (American). A small area around the Yangtze River basin in eastern China (Chinese).

Habitat
Freshwater swamps, marshes, lakes, rivers, and streams

Habits
Hunt mainly at night; unlike other reptiles, mother alligators tend their nests and raise their young

Diet
Fish, birds, snakes, and turtles; sometimes larger animals such as deer

Distinctive Features
Armor-plated body, short legs, long snout filled with sharp teeth

Fast Fact
Alligators are often referred to as gators.

Average Size

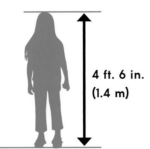

Human (age 10)

4 ft. 6 in.
(1.4 m)

American Alligator (adult)

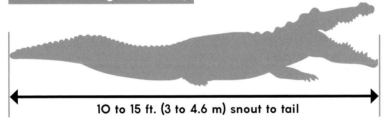

10 to 15 ft. (3 to 4.6 m) snout to tail

◀ A baby gator gets a ride from its mother.

Classification

CLASS
Reptilia
(reptiles)

ORDER
Crocodylia
(crocodilians)

FAMILY
Alligatoridae
(alligators and
caimans)

GENUS
Alligator
(alligator)

SPECIES
· *Alligator mississippiensis*
  (American)
· *Alligator sinensis*
  (Chinese)

CHAPTER 1

Powerful Predator

The sun is setting in Everglades

National Park in Florida. A bobcat heads to the edge of the swamp for a drink. The surface of the water is still and calm. The only slight disturbance is caused by what looks like a log floating slowly along. The bobcat dips its head to drink. Suddenly there is an explosion of water and sound. An alligator lunges, opens its mouth wide, and grabs the startled animal in its teeth. The huge **reptile** quickly drags its **prey** beneath the surface to drown it. Then it begins to spin around and around, tearing chunks off the cat.

The word *alligator* comes from the Spanish word for lizard: *lagarto*. But this powerful **predator** is more like a dinosaur than a lizard. Alligators are tough like dinosaurs. And both animals roamed the Earth at the same time. Unlike dinosaurs, though, gators survived the mass **extinction** that wiped out most animals on the planet 65 million years ago.

▶ Once the alligator clamped its jaws shut on this bobcat, escape was impossible.

Fast Fact
Some alligators live as far west as the state of Texas.

Wet and Wild

There are only two species of alligator: Chinese and American. American alligators are found only in the United States. They favor the warmer climate of the Southeast, with most making their home in Florida and Louisiana. Chinese alligators live in a small area along China's lower Yangtze River. They are critically endangered—fewer than 150 live in the wild today.

Alligators are semi-aquatic reptiles, moving periodically from water to land. They spend most of their time in freshwater habitats like swamps and marshes. They also live in and around lakes and slow-moving rivers. Gators can tolerate a little bit of salt water but not much. That's because alligators don't have salt glands to excrete salt from their bodies. Animals like sharks, rays, seabirds, and even some reptiles have salt glands.

◀ This is a photo of a Chinese alligator.

Cold-Blooded Critters

Alligators prefer to live in warm areas because, like all reptiles, they are ectotherms. That means they are cold-blooded. Warm-blooded animals (including people) can adjust their body temperature. Cold-blooded animals like alligators cannot. An alligator's body temperature depends on the temperature of its surroundings. To get warm, this huge reptile comes ashore to **bask** in the sun. If it gets too warm, the gator opens its mouth wide to release some heat. Other options for cooling down include moving into the shade or slipping back into the water.

Alligators are not very active in colder weather, but they can handle a chill. As long as a gator stays in the water, it can even survive freezing temperatures. The alligator just has to keep its nostrils above the surface. This way, even if the rest of its body is trapped beneath ice, the alligator can breathe.

▶ An alligator can breathe while most of its body is underwater.

Fast Fact
Alligators never stop growing.

King of the Reptiles

Alligators are the largest reptiles in North America. Males, called bulls, weigh between 500 and 600 pounds (226.8 and 272.2 kilograms). Females are usually a bit smaller. They average about 8.2 feet (2.6 meters) in length and weigh about half as much as males.

Chinese alligators are very similar to their American cousins. But there are a few differences, including size. Chinese alligators are smaller. They usually grow to about 5 ft. (1.5 m) and weigh less than 50 lb. (22.7 kg). A Chinese alligator's snout is a little different from an American gator's. The snout narrows toward the front and turns up a little at the end. In Chinese, the alligator is called *tulong*, which means "earth dragon."

◀ Unlike American alligators, Chinese alligators have bony plates in their eyelids.

Built Tough

Adult alligators usually have dark green or black bodies and a white belly. They are covered in scales, called scutes. The scutes act like a suit of armor—and they keep the alligator's skin from getting too dry. Gators have short legs and a long, powerful jaw that is filled with 80 teeth.

An alligator's eyes and nostrils are on the top of its head. That allows the animal to see and smell while the rest of its body is underwater. These nighttime hunters have a strong sense of smell and excellent hearing. Sensors on the alligator's skin help it detect movement in the water. If an animal disturbs the water at all, tiny black dots on the alligator's skin immediately pick up the vibration.

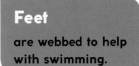

Feet
are webbed to help with swimming.

Fast Fact
Half of an alligator's length is in its tail.

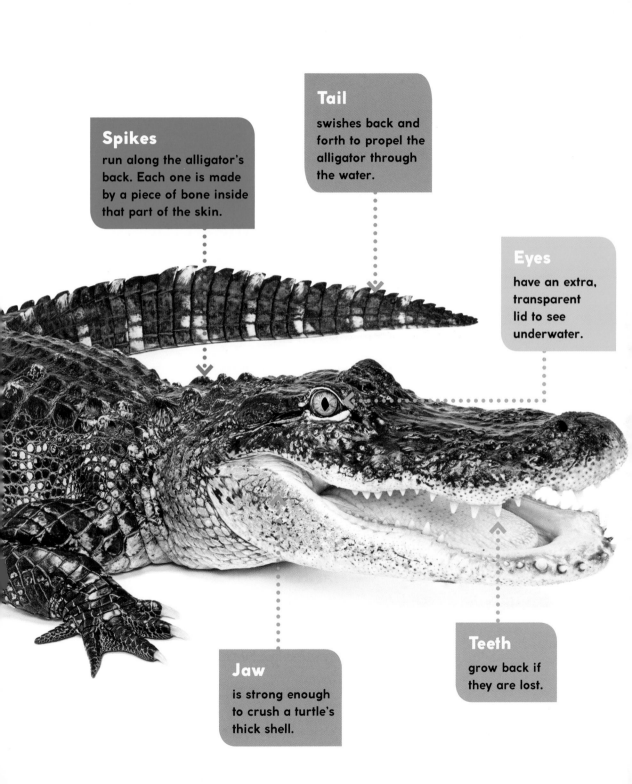

Spikes run along the alligator's back. Each one is made by a piece of bone inside that part of the skin.

Tail swishes back and forth to propel the alligator through the water.

Eyes have an extra, transparent lid to see underwater.

Jaw is strong enough to crush a turtle's thick shell.

Teeth grow back if they are lost.

CHAPTER 2

Swamp Life

Alligators are most at home in the water, and that's where they spend most of their time. When resting, alligators may float on the surface using water plants as buoys. At other times, they may lie at the bottom. An alligator at rest can stay below the surface for up to two hours. A typical dive—to look for food—may last up to 20 minutes.

When an alligator comes onto land, it may crawl, walk, or run to get around. An alligator's crawl is really more of a slither. Even when it's walking normally, this reptile usually stays pretty low to the ground, with its tail dragging behind. There is also something called "high" walking, during which the alligator lifts its tail and belly off the ground and walks on its toes. When running, an alligator stays pretty low to the ground, but that certainly doesn't slow it down. A running alligator can reach speeds of about 10 miles (16.1 kilometers) per hour.

▶ As the alligator crawls into a swamp, its tail swishes back and forth.

Roseate Spoonbill

▶ Wading birds must be alert, or they may become easy prey for an alligator.

Turtle

▶ Few animals other than gators have jaws strong enough to crush a turtle's shell.

Gopher Frog

▶ This amphibian lives in Florida—prime alligator country.

Northern Water Snake

▶ Alligators in the Carolinas are likely to feast on these snakes.

Sneak Attack

Alligators are carnivores, which means they eat meat. Adult alligators eat everything from fish, birds, snakes, and turtles to larger animals like small mammals. Adults will even eat baby gators!

An alligator could chase prey on land, but it would tire very quickly. This powerful predator does most of its hunting in the water. It is an ambush predator.

An alligator's coloring works as camouflage in its watery surroundings. In fact, if an alligator stays very still, it looks a lot like a drifting log. An alligator will remain motionless for hours if necessary while it waits for its prey to come closer.

When an alligator senses prey nearby, it sinks completely under the water. Its nostrils clamp closed so water can't get in. And a valve at the back of the alligator's throat closes to keep water out of its stomach and lungs. Then the gator lunges. SNAP! The alligator traps its prey between its teeth.

◀ Any animal that lives in or near the water is fair game to an American alligator!

Fast Fact
These meat-eaters
are also known
to eat fruit.

Mealtime

Alligators don't chew their food. If the prey is small, like a fish, the alligator will tilt its head back with its snout in the air and swallow the fish whole. If the prey is large, like a deer, the alligator will pull it underwater and then spin around and around with the prey in its mouth. When a chunk of meat rips off, the alligator will surface, look up, and swallow the chunk in one gulp. An alligator can digest anything it eats, including bones, so no part of the meal is ever wasted.

Cold-blooded animals like alligators don't use a lot of energy. So they don't need to eat very often. Alligators in the wild typically eat only once a week. But if necessary, a gator can go two years without eating. During that time, it lives off the fat reserves stored at the base of its tail.

◄ A small fish called a Florida gar is one of the American alligator's favorite foods.

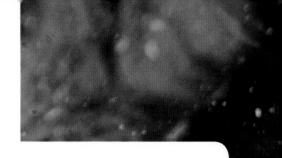

Now Hear This!

The American alligator is one of the most vocal reptiles on Earth. Alligators start making noises to communicate before they're even born! Baby alligators make chirping calls from inside their eggs.

Adult alligators make a roaring sound called a bellow. Scientists believe alligators make these noises to let other gators know where they are. Males may also use this sound to attract females. Alligators also hiss and make a coughing or purring sound called a chumpf. These sounds are often heard during the mating process.

Alligators also use other forms of communication. For example, a male may slap his head on the surface of the water to tell other males to back off. These remarkable reptiles also make noises that people can't hear. But we can see them—the vibrations cause the water around the gator's back to bubble and ripple.

▶ Can you see the ripples this alligator is making in the water?

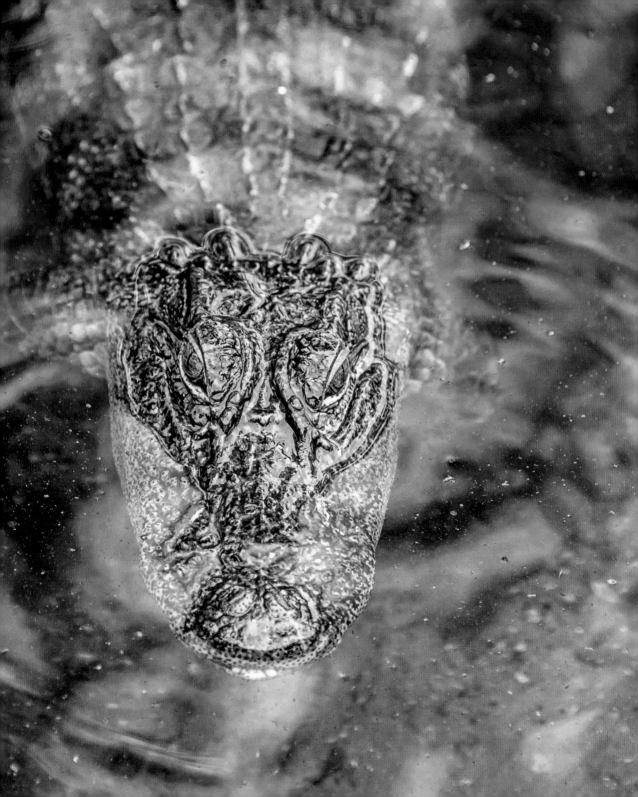

Time to Slow Down

Alligators don't **hibernate** in winter, but they do slow down if the weather gets too cold. Alligators stop eating once the temperature dips below 70°F (21.1°C). If the temperature drops below 55°F (12.8°C), an alligator may become **dormant**.

First the gator makes a **burrow** near a water source. The burrow consists of a tunnel that leads to a den. The den must be above water level so the gator can breathe. Then the alligator settles in to rest. It doesn't move much at all. But if the weather warms up, the gator may leave its burrow to bask in the sun. It may even slip into the water to hunt.

Sometimes alligators create their own water source, called a gator hole, near the burrow. The alligator clears the mud and plants from an area of land. Then the hole fills up with rainwater. Water usually stays in gator holes even during a **drought**. During this time, gator holes may be the only water source for the animals in the area.

◀ **An alligator basks in the warm sunlight.**

CHAPTER 3

Growing Up Gator

Both male and female alligators are mature enough to **mate** when they reach 6 ft. (1.8 m) in length. That usually happens when the animal is around 10 to 12 years old. Alligators start looking for mates in April. To attract females, males bellow and stir up the water with head slaps. They also do this to discourage other males from coming around. If a male tries to enter another bull's **territory** during mating season, it can end in a fight.

By May, the animals have chosen their mates. The alligators may rub against each other, blow bubbles, and make purring sounds. The male may even lift his head out of the water and expose his neck to show the female that he means no harm. Mating takes place at night in shallow water. When it is over, the bull goes off to mate with other females.

▶ **The winner of this fight will get the chance to mate with a female.**

A Cozy Nest

By June a pregnant female alligator is busily building a nest. She makes it out of grass and mud. Like all reptiles, alligators lay eggs. The eggs would not survive underwater, so the alligator builds the nest on dry land. It can be 3 ft. (0.9 m) high and 6 ft. (1.8 m) across. The female lays 20 to 50 eggs in a hole at the top of the nest and then covers it up with grass. As the vegetation rots, it creates heat to keep the eggs warm. The temperature inside the nest determines whether baby gators will be male or female. If the temperature is very warm, most of the babies will be female. If it's cooler, most will be male.

Unlike most reptiles, the mother alligator stays close to the nest. She has to guard it from predators like raccoons. There is one animal that is often successful at raiding the nest, though. Red turtles often sneak into alligator nests to lay their own eggs. It's a great way to guarantee their safety!

◀ Even though you can't see her, you can be sure the mother gator is not far from her nest!

Hatching Time

Toward the end of August, the young alligators are ready to hatch. They start making chirping noises from inside their eggs. When the mother alligator hears the sound, she begins digging through the nest to expose the eggs. The baby gators break through their shells using their heads and a special egg tooth on their snouts. If a baby is having trouble hatching, though, the mother gator will help. She will pick up the egg in her mouth and use her tongue to gently roll it against the roof of her mouth until it finally cracks.

The babies, which are now called hatchlings, are 6 to 8 inches (15.2 to 20.3 centimeters) long and have black and yellow stripes. The mother gator picks up about 10 hatchlings at a time in her mouth and carries them to the water. Then she opens her mouth and shakes her head gently back and forth to encourage the hatchlings to swim out into their new home.

▶ **By the time the babies are ready to hatch, the eggs are soft like leather.**

Safety in Numbers

Hatchlings are able to hunt as soon as they are born. They feed on crayfish, insects, small fish, and shrimp. Young gators grow fast in their first years of life—up to one foot a year. But they are too small to live on their own. Young alligators may live together with their siblings and their mother in a group, called a pod, for up to three years.

The hatchlings' yellow and black coloring helps them blend in among the water plants where they live. If a young alligator gets into trouble, its chirps will bring its mother swimming to the rescue. Alligators are one of the only reptiles that actually take care of their young.

Still only about one in five hatchlings survives to adulthood. They can fall prey to birds, raccoons, or even adult alligators. If the youngsters do manage to survive, they may live up to 50 years in the wild.

◀ A pod can contain up to 50 hatchlings.

CHAPTER 4

Living Dinosaurs

The alligator can trace its roots all the way back to a group of ancient reptiles called crocodylomorpha. They lived more than 205 million years ago. This group included a massive creature called *Deinosuchus*. Other than being 40 ft. (12.2 m) long, *Deinosuchus* looked a lot like its modern cousins the gators. Scientists say this massive predator sat comfortably at the top of the food chain. It was not hunted by any other animal. There is even evidence to suggest that *Deinosuchus* preyed on dinosaurs!

The alligator **ancestor** most like today's gator was *Brachychampsa*, which lived 80 million years ago. It is the earliest known meat-eating reptile to live in fresh water. And it looked almost exactly like modern alligators. No wonder gators look like creatures from another time. They are!

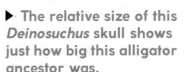

▶ **The relative size of this *Deinosuchus* skull shows just how big this alligator ancestor was.**

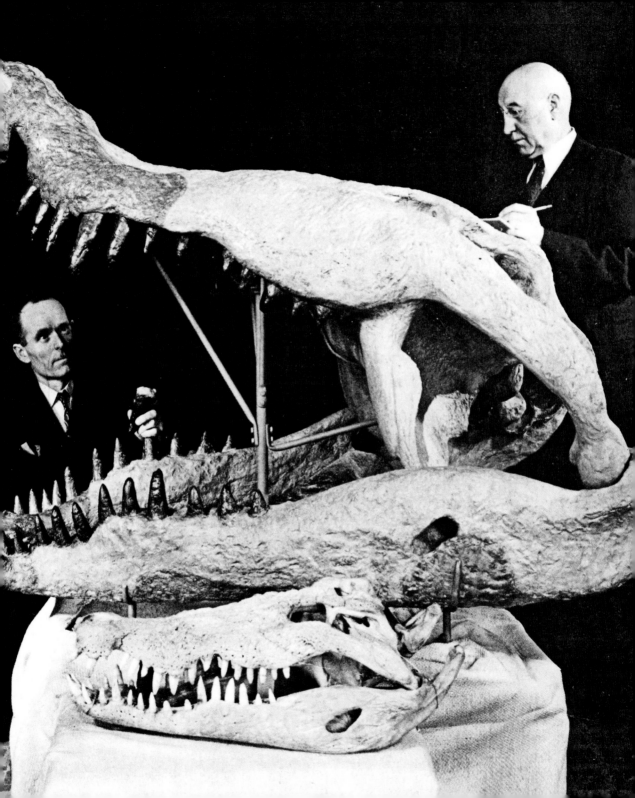

Reptilian Relatives

Alligators are part of a group called crocodilians. More than half the reptiles in the group are crocodiles. The "non-crocodiles" include five species of caimans, two alligators, and one gharial. The main difference between most of these animals is where they live. Caimans are found in Central and South America. The gharial, which lives in India and Nepal, looks a bit different from the rest.

Likewise, the biggest different between alligators and crocodiles is where they live. Crocs like it hot. Their northern range limit is southern Florida. In fact, that is the only place on Earth where alligators and crocodiles live together. It can be hard to tell alligators and crocodiles apart just by looking at them. But it's possible if you look closely! An alligator has a rounded U-shaped snout. A crocodile has a long V-shaped snout. When an alligator's mouth is closed, only its top teeth show. When a crocodile's mouth is closed, all of its teeth show. An alligator's skin is darker than a crocodile's, which may be green, gray, or even brown.

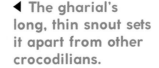

◀ The gharial's long, thin snout sets it apart from other crocodilians.

CHAPTER 5

Living with Gators

Ten million American alligators were killed over the course of 100 years—from 1870 to 1970. People hunted them for their meat. But they also killed alligators for their skin, which is very tough and was valued for making shoes, belts, and handbags.

Then, in 1967, the alligator was listed as endangered under the Endangered Species Preservation Act. This law was followed by the Endangered Species Act of 1973. These laws were created to protect animals that are at risk of becoming extinct. It is illegal to kill or hurt animals protected by these laws.

Despite these protections, people continued to hunt alligators illegally. In the mid-1970s, new laws that punished people for trading alligator skins helped bring the alligator back from the brink. Today, more than one million wild alligators live in the United States.

▶ In many places, it is once again legal to trade allligator skins.

A Delicate Balance

Alligators were removed from the list of endangered animals in 1987. But they still face serious challenges to their survival.

Every year the alligators' habitat shrinks a little more as people fill **wetlands** with rocks and dirt to make dry land. Then they build houses and towns right where the alligators used to live. At best, the alligators must find somewhere else to live. At worst, they can be killed when they wander onto a golf course or into a housing development.

The alligators' survival is crucial to their entire **ecosystem**. Many animals rely on gator holes during dry seasons. And new plants and trees often grow up from abandoned alligator nests. This creates habitats for all sorts of wildlife. Just as important, the alligator is an American icon. It is a symbol of the raw wild beauty of untamed nature. Alligators have survived for millions of years. It would be a shame if humans were to blame for ending their time on Earth.

◀ Alligator sightings are not uncommon on Florida's golf courses.

Alligator Family Tree

Alligators are a type of crocodilian. Like all crocodilians, they are reptiles. Reptiles are cold-blooded animals that crawl across the ground or creep on short legs. They have backbones and most reproduce by laying eggs. This diagram shows how alligators are related to other crocodilians and animals that are descended from reptiles. The closer together two animals are on the tree, the more similar they are.

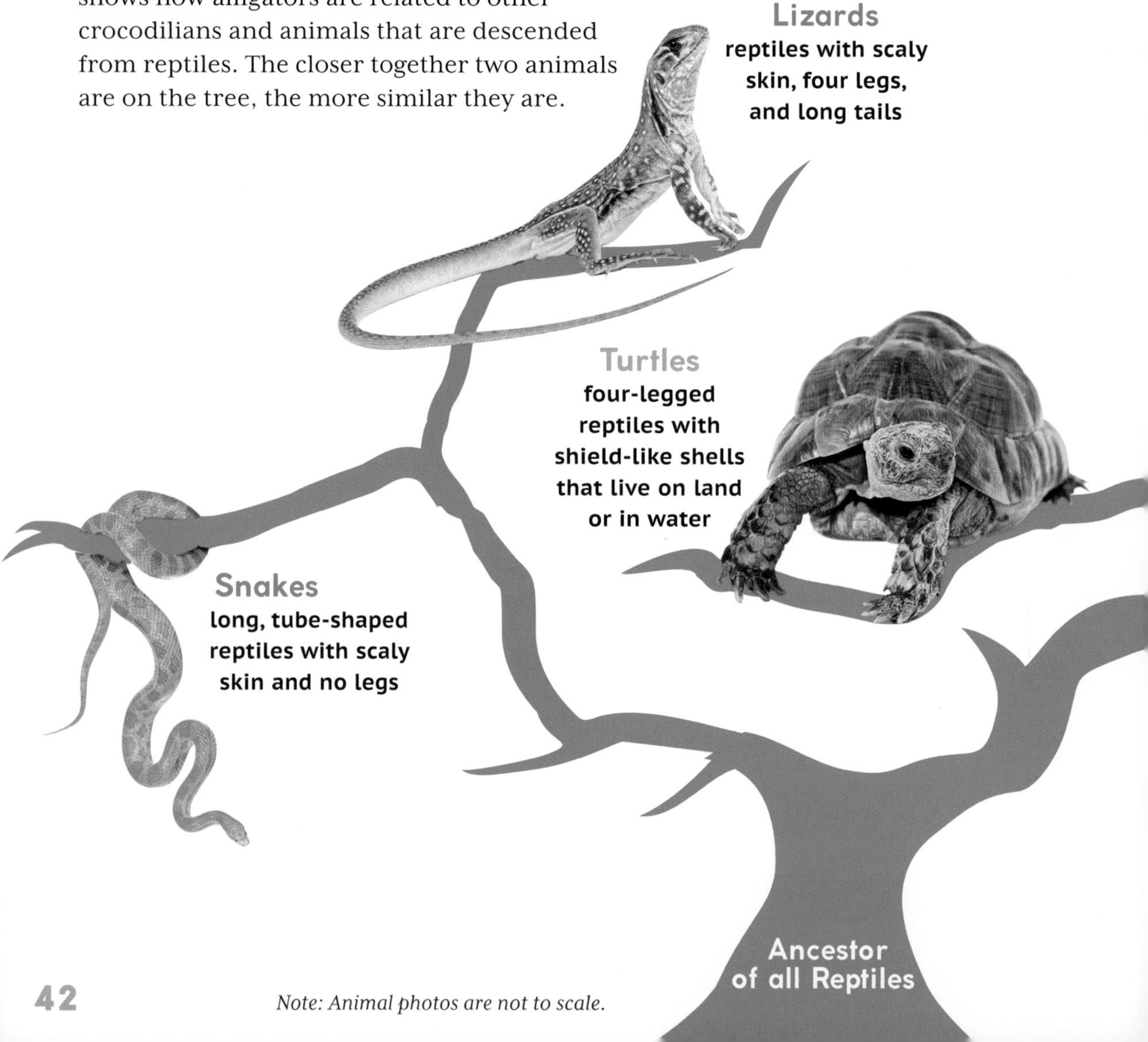

Lizards
reptiles with scaly skin, four legs, and long tails

Turtles
four-legged reptiles with shield-like shells that live on land or in water

Snakes
long, tube-shaped reptiles with scaly skin and no legs

Ancestor of all Reptiles

Note: Animal photos are not to scale.

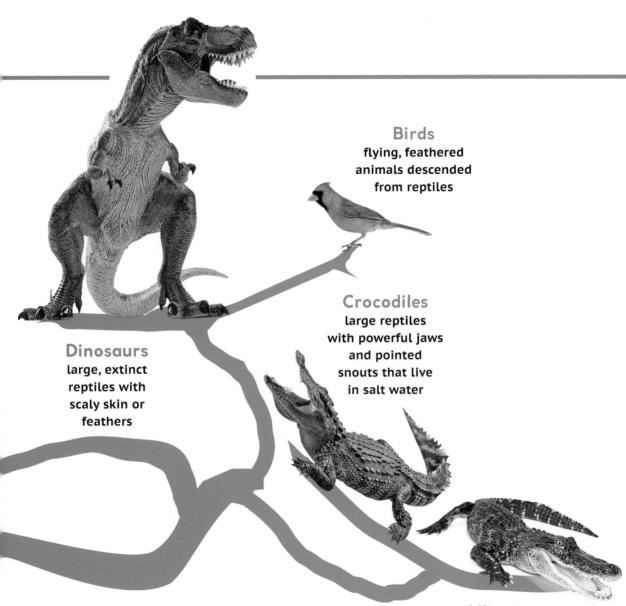

Birds
flying, feathered
animals descended
from reptiles

Crocodiles
large reptiles
with powerful jaws
and pointed
snouts that live
in salt water

Dinosaurs
large, extinct
reptiles with
scaly skin or
feathers

Alligators
large reptiles
with powerful
jaws and rounded
snouts that live
in fresh water

Words to Know

A .... **ambush** *(AM-bush)* to attack from a hiding place

ancestor *(ANN-ses-tur)* a family member who lived long ago

B .... **bask** *(BASK)* to lie or sit in the sun for pleasure

burrow *(BUR-oh)* a tunnel or hole in the ground made or used as a home by an animal

C .... **camouflage** *(KAM-uh-flahzh)* a way of hiding by using coloring, pattern, or shape to blend into one's surroundings

climate *(KLYE-mit)* the weather typical of a place over a long period of time

D .... **dormant** *(DOR-muhnt)* not active, but capable of becoming active

drought *(DROUT)* a long period without rain

E .... **ecosystem** *(EE-koh-sis-tuhm)* all the living things in a place and their relation to their environment

endangered *(en-DAYN-juhrd)* a plant or animal that is in danger of becoming extinct, usually because of human activity

excrete *(ik-SKREET)* get rid of waste matter or other substances from the body

extinction *(ik-STINGK-shun)* the act of killing off a species

G .... **glands** *(GLANDZ)* organs in the body that produce or release natural chemicals

H .... **habitats** *(HAB-i-tats)* the place where an animal or plant is usually found

hibernate *(HYE-bur-nayt)* when animals hibernate, they sleep for the entire winter

M .... **mammals** *(MAM-uhlz)* warm-blooded animals that have hair or fur and usually give birth to live babies; female mammals produce milk to feed their young

mate *(MATE)* to join together for breeding

P .... **predator** *(PRED-uh-tuhr)* an animal that lives by hunting other animals for food

prey *(PRAY)* an animal that is hunted by another animal for food

R .... **reptile** *(REP-tile)* a cold-blooded animal that crawls across the ground or creeps on short legs; it has a backbone and most reproduce by laying eggs

S .... **semi-aquatic** *(SEM-ee-uh-KWAT-ik)* living or growing partly on land and partly in water

sensors *(SEN-surz)* instruments that can detect and measure changes and transmit the information to a controlling device

species *(SPEE-sheez)* one of the groups into which animals and plants are divided; members of the same species can mate and have offspring

T .... **territory** *(TER-i-tor-ee)* an area that an animal or group of animals uses and defends

V .... **vibration** *(vye-BRAY-shuhn)* the feeling or sensation of something moving back and forth rapidly

W .... **wetlands** *(WET-landz)* land where there is a lot of moisture in the soil; these include swamps, bayous, and marshes

Find Out More

BOOKS

- Furstinger, Nancy. *Alligators (Amazing Reptiles)*. Mankato, MN: ABDO, 2015.
- Hirsch, Rebecca E. *American Alligators: Armored Roaring Reptiles*. New York: Lerner Publications, 2016.
- Riggs, Kate. *Alligators (Amazing Animals Series)*. Mankato, MN: The Creative Company, 2012.

WEB PAGES

- www.arkive.org/american-alligator/alligator-mississippiensis/
  Photos and information about the American alligator from Arkive, a wildlife database created by the British educational charity Wildscreen.
- www.nationalgeographic.com/animals/reptiles/a/american-alligator/
  Fascinating facts about the alligator from National Geographic.
- www.nps.gov/ever/learn/nature/alligator.htm
  In-depth information from the Everglades National Park Web site.

Facts for Now

Visit this Scholastic Web site for more information on alligators:
www.factsfornow.scholastic.com Enter the keyword Alligators

Index

Index *(continued)*

About the Author

Stephanie Fitzgerald is the author of numerous
nonfiction books for kids. She especially enjoys
learning and writing about all types of animals ...
except maybe spiders. Stephanie lives in Connecticut
with her husband and her hatchling, Molly.